Long

Popcorn

3

Pupils' Book

Brian Abbs • Anne Worrall • Ann Ward

Ben's new friend

 Listen and look.

It's Saturday morning. The Taylor family are having breakfast.

 Practice with your friends.

1 Cody's furniture

 Listen and point.

 Talk to your friend.

 What's this? It's Cody's closet.

2 An Australian family

 Talk to your friend.

 Who's this?

It's Cody's brother.

3 Where are they from?

 Talk to your friend.

Where's Andrew from?

He's from Australia.

 Where are you from? Talk to your friend.

4 Moving Day!

Rhyme.

Our chairs are in the bathroom.
My bed is in the hall.
The couch is in the kitchen,
But where's my ball?

The fridge is in the yard,
The closet's on the stairs,
The writing desk is upside down,
But where are my bears?

Find the ball and the teddy bears.

2 At the swimming pool

Listen and look.

It's Sunday. The Taylor family, Jill, Cody and Todd are at the swimming pool.

2

 Practice with your friends.

Tell Sally and Todd what to do.

 Sally, take off Mary's shoes.

 Todd, put on your jacket.

2

1 What are they wearing?

Look at the pictures.

 Talk to your friend.

What's Mary wearing?   She's wearing Jill's sweater.

 What are you wearing? Talk to your friend.

2 Days of the week

 Listen and say.

Monday — wash the car

Tuesday — wash the dishes

Wednesday — swim in the ocean

Thursday — do his homework

Friday — play soccer

Saturday — walk in the park

Sunday — read a book

I ♥ the weekend

 Read about Cody's friend Mick. Talk to your friend.

What day is it today?

It's Monday.

What's Mick doing?

He's washing the car.

2

3 Swimming race

Choose a lane and answer the questions.

Dive in here!

Lane 1

1 What's your name?

2 Do you like spiders?

3 What color is this?

4 What's this?

5 Where is Cody from?

6 Does he have a plane?

Lane 2

1 How old are you?

2 Do you like cats?

3 What color is this?

4 What's this?

5 How old is Cody?

6 Does she have a car?

Lane 3

1 Where do you live?

2 Do you like snails?

3 What color is this?

4 What's this?

5 What color is Cody's jacket?

6 Does he have an apple?

Lane 4

1 What's your favorite food?

2 Do you like dogs?

3 What color is this?

4 What's this?

5 Is Cody a good swimmer?

6 Does she have a pencil?

FINISH

How do you spell it?

 Listen and look.

 Practice with your friends.

1   A map of Australia

Listen and find the places.

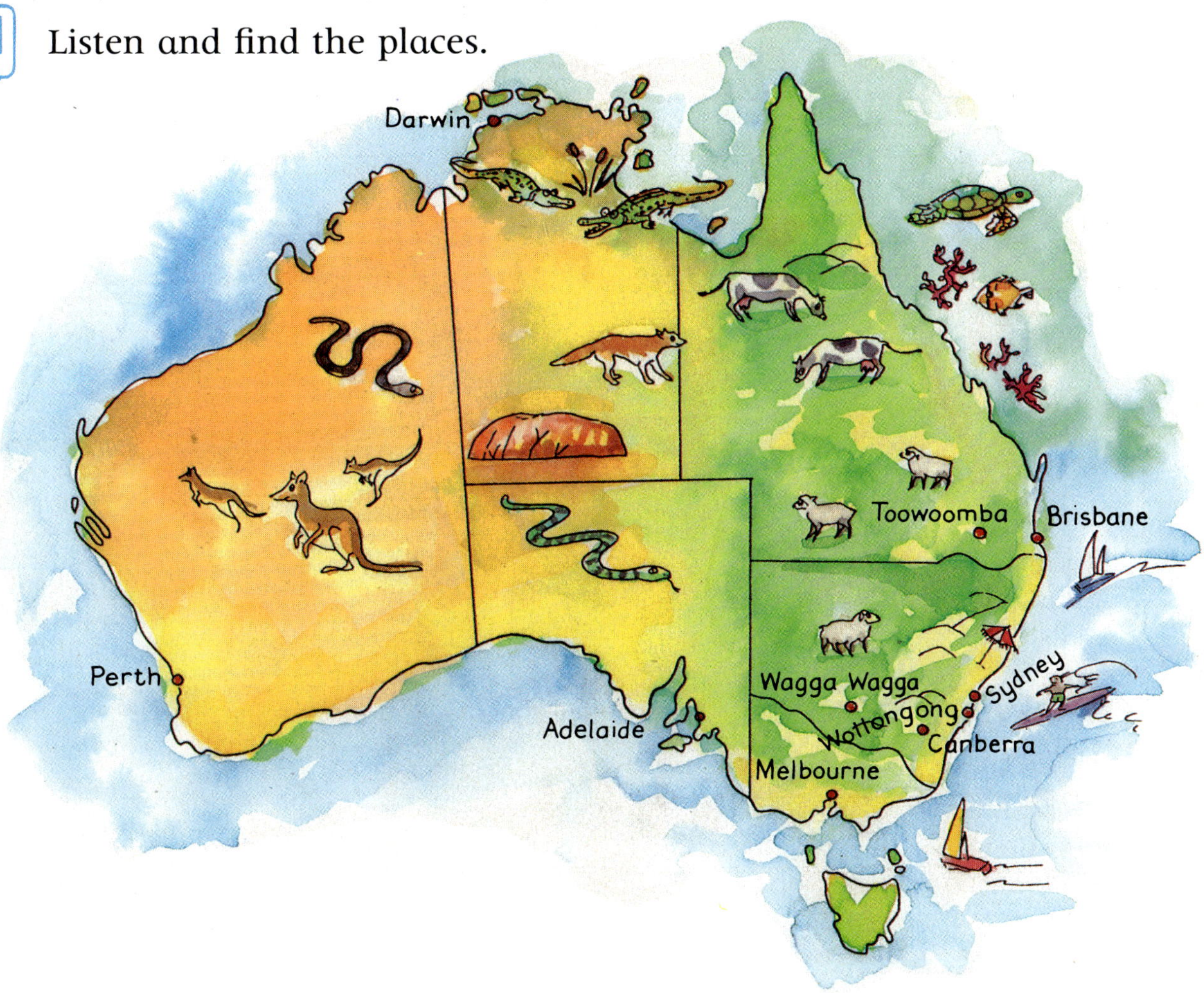

2 The Alphabet

Listen and say.

A B C D E F G H I J K L M
N O P Q R S T U V W X Y Z

3 How do you spell it?

Listen and point.

Talk to your friend.

(What's this?) (It's a pencil.) (How do you spell it?) (P–E–N–C–I–L.)

4 I spy with my little eye

Game. Look at the picture.

I spy with my little eye
something beginning with C.

5 Can you spell hat?

Song.

Can you spell hat?
Can you spell cat?
And how many Ns in Jenny?
Can you spell right?
There's a G in right.
And there are two Ns in Jenny.
Yes, there are two Ns in Jenny.

So, hey, hey, It's the alphabet.
Spelling in English is fun!
A's before B,
After that there is C,
And Y's the last letter
But one, but one,
Oh, spelling in English is fun!

Can you spell nice?
And twice and mice?
And how many Ns in Jenny?
Can you spell Joe?
There's an E in Joe.
And there are two Ns in Jenny.
Yes, there are two Ns in Jenny.

6 How many letters are there?

Look at the name of this town in Wales, in Britain.

LLANFAIRPWLLGWYNGYLLGOGERYCHWYRNDROBWLLLLANTYSILIOGOGOGOCH

Talk to your friend.

How many Y's are there?

Five.

13

thirteen

4 A project about Australia

 Listen and look.

The capital of Australia is Canberra but this is a photo of my favorite city – Sydney. Sydney is famous for its bridge and its Opera House.

Aborigines are the original Australian people. These children live in Alice Springs. Alice Springs is in the middle of Australia. It is in the desert.

Australia is a very beautiful continent. There are lots of interesting animals. This is a kangaroo and her baby. Kangaroos live in the outback.

4

Crocodiles live in the outback too.

There are a lot of farms in Australia. These sheep live on a big farm in the middle of Australia. The farm is called a sheep station.

Some people live in the outback very far from the towns. This flying doctor is visiting people on a farm by plane.

Australia is famous for its beaches. You can swim in the sea and surf or go diving. It's great fun!

 Look at the photos of Australia. Which is your favorite photo? Talk to your friend.

1 Australian animals

Look at the photos. Listen and point.

jump

swim

climb

run

walk

sleep

dingo
(wild dog)

kangaroo

koala

wombat

crocodile

platypus

2 What are they doing?

Talk to your friend.

 What's this?

It's a kangaroo.

 What's it doing?

It's jumping.

3 Find the animal

Read and match.

This animal is tall. It has a long tail. It has two long legs and two short legs. It has big ears. It has strong back legs.

This animal has a long body and short legs. It has a long mouth. It has small eyes.

It doesn't have any ears.

 Choose an animal. Talk to your friend.

4   Australia quiz

Answer these questions about Australia with your friend.

1   What's the capital of Australia?

2   Where is this Opera House?

3   Where is Alice Springs?

4   What is a sheep station?

5   What is this animal?

6   Who are Aborigines?

7   What are these people doing?

8   What is a dingo?

Make a quiz about your country with your friends.

5   Guess the animal!

Game. Think of an animal.
Act it out. Your partner guesses.

5 A shapes jungle

 Practice with your friends.

5

1 Shapes

Listen and point.

Talk to your friend.

What's this?

It's a square.

What color is it?

It's blue.

2 Shape pictures

Tell your friend how to draw these pictures.

Draw a circle for the head.

Add eight triangles for the hair.

3 One, two, buckle my shoe

Rhyme.

One, two, buckle my shoe,
Three, four, knock at the door,
Five, six, pick up sticks,
Seven, eight, open the gate,
Nine, ten, a big fat hen,
Eleven, twelve, dig and delve,
Thirteen, fourteen, maids a-courting,
Fifteen, sixteen, maids in the kitchen.
Seventeen, eighteen, maids a-waiting.
Nineteen, twenty, my plate's empty!

4 How many can you see?

Ask your friend.

How many triangles are there in the picture?   There are nineteen.

 **6** # What can you do?

 Listen and look.

Miss Fisher is talking to Ben's class.

 Practice with your friends.

6

1 What can they do?

 Listen and point.

play the piano

sing

play the drums

dance

play the recorder

play the guitar

ride a bike

cook

 Talk to your friend.

Can Sally ride a bike? No.

What can Tom do? He can cook.

6

2 I can be anything

Song.

When I'm playing I pretend,
And when I pretend, I can be anything!
I can be a crocodile, with great, big, yellow eyes.
I can be an eagle, flying through the skies.
I can be an elephant.
I can be a snake.
I can be a tiger.
I can be anything . . .

3 Who am I?

Game. Choose a picture. Don't tell your partner.

name: Andrew
age: 10
can: play the piano, cook, swim, ride a bike
likes: horses, books

name: Anna
age: 10
can: dance, ride a bike, sing, cook
likes: dogs, books

name: Claire
age: 10
can: play soccer, ride a bike, sing, play the piano
likes: dogs, music

name: Robert
age: 10
can: play the piano, dance, play soccer, swim
likes: music, horses

Your partner asks questions. Look at your picture.
Answer the questions.

Can you play football?

Yes.

Can you ride a bike?

No.

7 It's snowing!

Listen and look.

 Practice with your friends.

7

1   What's the weather like?

Listen and point.

It's hot and sunny.

It's snowing.

It's raining.

It's windy.

It's cloudy.

It's cold.

Read and match.

We can have a picnic.

I can fly my kite.

I can't see the sun.

We can't play soccer.

We can build a snowman.

I can't swim in the ocean.

Talk to your friend.

What's the weather like?

It's snowing. We can build a snowman!

It's raining. We can't play soccer!

2 Rainy Day Robin

Song.

I am standing alone by the window.
I am watching the rain come splashing down.
I am watching the people holding their umbrellas.
They don't like the rain which is coming down
All over the town.

I am Rainy Day Robin,
I like watching the rain.
I know I can't play in the park today
But I'm happy just watching the rain.

Are you like Rainy Day Robin?
Do you like watching the rain?
When you know you can't play in the park today?
Are you happy just watching the rain?

I am Rainy Day Robin,
I like watching the rain.
I know I can't play in the park today
But I'm happy just watching the rain.
The lovely, beautiful rain.
I'm happy just watching the rain.

3 The weather today

Draw a picture of the weather today.
Talk to your friend.

8 Shopping!

 Listen and look.

This store is called a bakery.
It sells bread and cakes.

This is a bookstore. You can buy
comic books and magazines here.

This is a flower store. You can
buy flowers here.

This is a toy store. It sells all kinds
of toys.

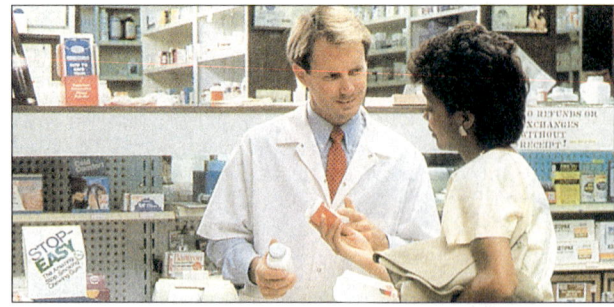

This is a drugstore. You can buy
medicine here. You can buy soap
and shampoo, too.

This is a big supermarket. You
can buy all kinds of food here.

8

1 Where can you buy a doll?

Look at the pictures.

a hot dog

a comic book

a doll

some cake

some jelly

some soap

some bread

some cheese

some toothpaste

some flowers

some books

some cookies

Talk to your friend.

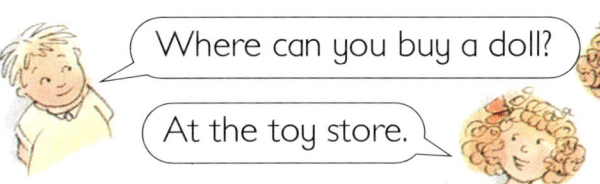

Where can you buy a doll?

At the toy store.

Where can you buy some cheese?

At the supermarket.

2 Which store are they in?

Listen and point.

FLOWER STORE   BAKERY   BOOKSTORE   DRUGSTORE   TOY STORE   SUPERMARKET

8

3 Numbers

Listen and say.

20 21 22 23 24 25 26 27 28
29 30 40 50 60 70 80 90 100

Listen and point.

4 How much is that?

Talk to your friend.

Can I have some bread, please?

Yes. Here you are.

Thank you. How much is that?

75 cents, please.

75¢

$1·00

$1·18

$1·69

33¢ a pound

95¢

99¢

$2·00

COMIC

50¢

CHIPS

75¢

candy

5 Whose basket is it?

Look at the pictures. Read and match.

① ② ④ ③

Tim has some oranges and some apples. He has some cheese. He likes cheese. He doesn't have any milk. He has some toothpaste and some soap.

Sarah has some oranges and some grapes. She doesn't have a doll. She doesn't like milk. She has some soap. She has some apples and some biscuits.

Sally has some cheese and some milk. She doesn't have any apples. She doesn't like apples. She has some toothpaste and a doll. She has some oranges.

Robert has some cheese and some apples. He doesn't like grapes. He has some milk. He doesn't have any oranges. He has some cookies.

6 A shopping game

Play this game with your friend.

I'm going shopping and I'm going to buy an apple.

I'm going shopping and I'm going to buy an apple and a banana.

I'm going shopping and I'm going to buy an apple, a banana and a car.

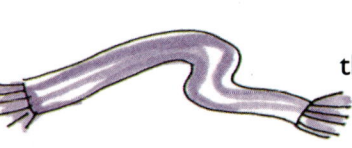

9 Can you ride a bicycle?

Listen and look.

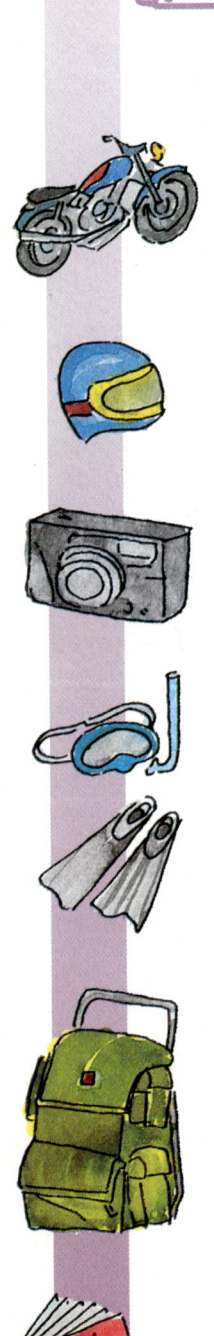

 Practice with your friends.

 What can your family do? Talk to your friend.

9

1 Fido the Great!

Look at the pictures. Listen and point.

① fly

② ride a horse

③ swim

④ surf

⑤ play basketball

⑥ ski

⑦ play tennis

⑧ play soccer

Talk to your friend about what Fido can and can't do.

 Fido can fly. He can't ski.

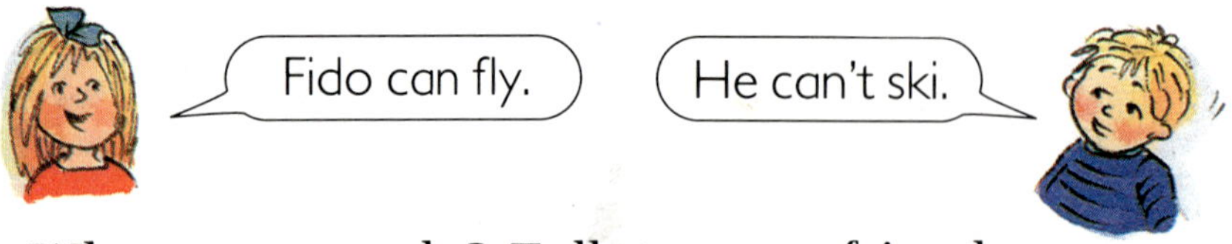

 What can you do? Talk to your friend.

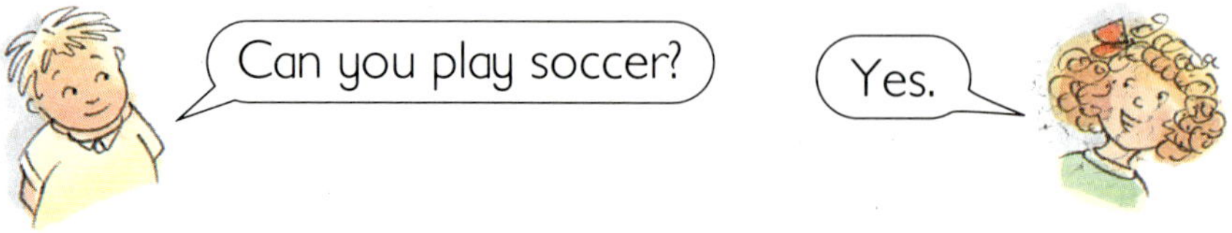

 Can you play soccer? Yes.

9

2 Answer the questions

Play the game with your friend.

START

Can you draw a square? ①

Can you draw a circle? ①

② Can you spell

Can you spell ②

③ Can you count to twenty?

Can you say the alphabet? ③

④ Can you say his name?

Can you say her name? ④

⑤ Can you make a word from these letters? ROHSE

Can you make a word from these letters? LOOCHS ⑤

⑥ Can you draw a crocodile?

Can you draw an elephant? ⑥

FINISH

37

thirty-seven

10 Making pancakes!

Put the flour in the bowl.
Add a little salt.

Add the egg and the milk.

Mix it with a spoon.

Heat some butter
in a frying pan.

Cook the pancakes.

Turn the pancakes over.
Be careful!

 Practice with your friends.

1 What are they doing?

 Look at the pictures. Talk to your friend.

 What's Ben doing in picture 4? He's putting the flour in the bowl.

2 Find the pancakes

Read and match.

Ben's pancake is small and thick. It's hard, too.

Jill's pancake is beautiful and thin. It's delicious.

Cody's pancake is very big. It's sticky, too.

Tom's pancake is on the floor. It's dirty but Mozart likes it.

 Talk to your friend.

 Whose pancake is number 1? It's Cody's.

3 It's sticky!

 Look at the pictures. Listen and point.

 Talk to your friend.

 Is number 1 sticky? No.

4   What do they need?

Look at the picture and read the
recipe for chocolate cake.

Chocolate cake
You need:
flour   a bowl
sugar   a spoon
an egg   a cake pan
butter
chocolate
1. Put the sugar and butter in a bowl.
2. Mix them together with a spoon.
3. Add the egg.
4. Add the flour and mix together.
5. Heat the chocolate and add to the bowl.
6. Cook the cake in the stove for 45 minutes.

Talk to your friend about the
things in the picture.

Do they need any eggs?

Yes.

Do they need a frying pan?

No.

5   Where are they?

Look at the picture again. Talk to your friend.

 Where's the flour?

It's on the shelf.

 Where are the eggs?

They're in the fridge.

 What can you cook? Talk to your friend.

What time is it?

 Listen and look.

It's Monday morning. Ben's family is in a hurry.

 Practice with your friends.

1 What time is it?

 Listen and point.

   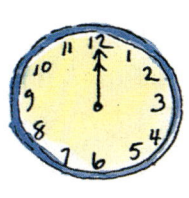  

Read and match.

It's twelve o'clock.   It's five-thirty.   It's ten-thirty.
It's two o'clock.   It's four-thirty.   It's eleven o'clock.

 Talk to your friend.

 What time is it?   It's four-thirty.

2 What time do you have breakfast?

Look at the pictures.

Read and match.

It's breakfast time.   It's snack time.
It's lunchtime.   It's bedtime.
It's dinner time.

 What time do you have breakfast?
What time do you go to bed?
Talk to your friend.

3 Let's have breakfast!

Game.

A = one-thirty
B = three-thirty
C = eight o'clock
D = ten o'clock
E = six-thirty
F = five o'clock

A = have dinner
B = have breakfast
C = go to bed
D = play a game
E = have lunch
F = climb a mountain

Spin the spinners. Talk to your friend. Is it a good idea?

It's one-thirty.
Let's have breakfast!
No!

It's eight o'clock.
Let's have dinner!
Yes!

4 We like eating spaghetti!

Song.

Tick-tick-tock, we can hear the clock,
It will soon be time for dinner.
By half past eight it will be on the plate,
But there's time for a song before dinner.

Oh, we like eating spaghetti.
We like the way that it curls
Round a spoon or a fork,
Suck it in as you talk,
And twist it in circles and whirls.

Oh, we like eating spaghetti.
It doesn't stay long on our plates.
Twist it once and then twice,
With tomatoes it's nice.
Oh, eating spaghetti is great!

12 Let's watch TV!

This woman is reading the television news.

Do you like cartoons? They are funny. They make you laugh.

There are lots of exciting movies on television. This is an adventure movie.

Do you like sports? This is a football game.

You can see your favorite pop singers on music programs.

This is the weather forecast. The man is talking about tomorrow's weather.

1 What's on TV?

Look at the television page.

25	26	27	28
5:30 The news	5:30 Cartoon time	5:30 Music for you	6:00 The news
6:00 Movie: Adventure in Space	6:00 The news	6:30 Soccer game	7:00 Movie: Where is Susan?
	6:30 Weather forecast		

 Talk to your friends about the television programs.

What's on Channel 25 at five-thirty?

The news.

2 What do you want to watch?

 Look at the television page. Talk to your friend.

What do you want to watch?

Cartoon time.

What time is it on?

Five-thirty.

 What's your favorite TV program?
Talk to your friend.

3　Jill's favorite cartoon

Jill's favorite cartoon
is the Rodeo Bunch.

 Who is she describing?
Listen and point.

4　Cold in winter

 Song.

Do you sometimes stop and wonder
About the things that you really like?
Your favorite food and your favorite color,
The wind in your hair
When you're riding your bike?

What things do you like?
When it's cold in winter,
After school when you're home and free,
I wonder . . .
Do you like the same things as I do?
Tea and cheese sandwiches and watching TV?

TV, tea and cheese sandwiches, a cushion to lie on the floor.
TV, tea and cheese sandwiches, I don't want any more.
But yes, there's something I need.
I must have something to read.
Turn off the TV. There's nothing to see.
Please give me my tea and lovely cheese sandwiches.
And something exciting to read.

13 At the fair

 Listen and look.

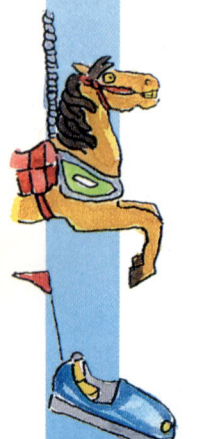

13

1   What can you do at the fair?

 Listen and point.

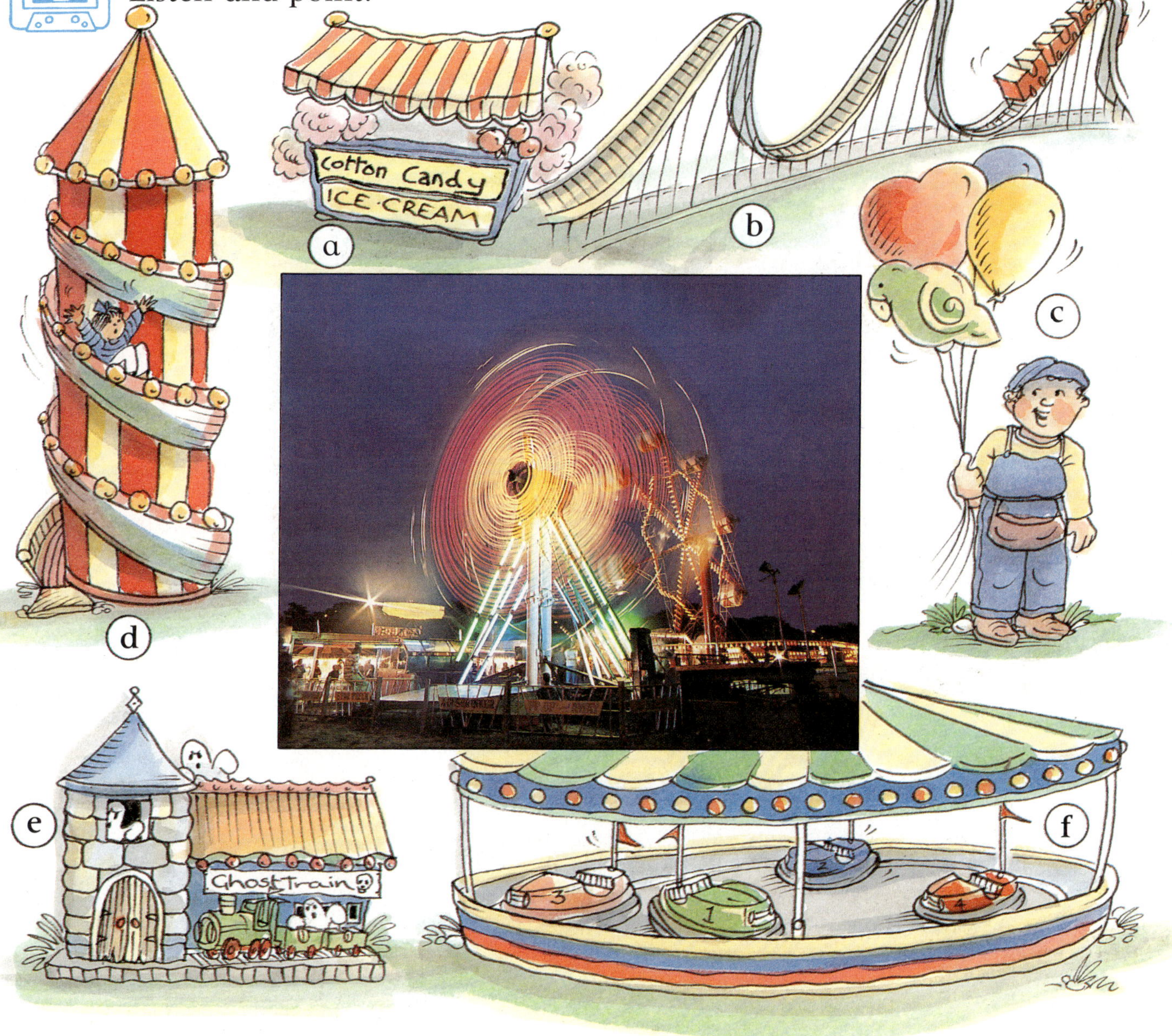

a

b

c

d

e

f

2   What do you want to do?

 Talk to your friend.

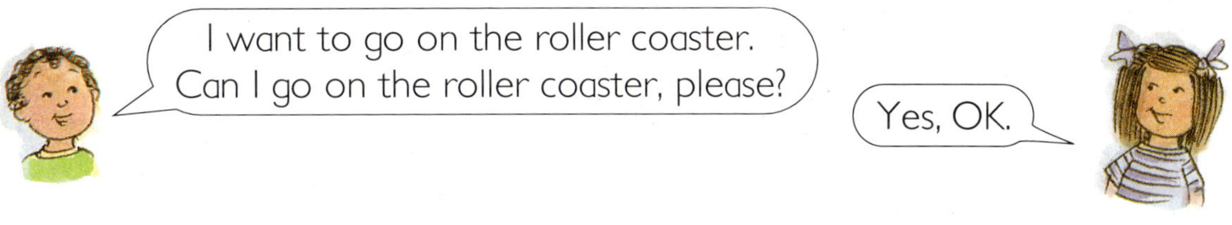

I want to go on the roller coaster.
Can I go on the roller coaster, please?

Yes, OK.

49
forty-nine

3 How do they feel?

 Look and say.

| hungry | tired | sick | frightened | thirsty | excited |

Eddy is hungry.

4 In the hall of mirrors

 Listen and point.

Ask your partner.

 Who's short and fat?

 Who's tall and thin?

 Who has a big head and a small body?

13

5   On the ghost train

Listen and read.

creepy crawly tunnel

The ghost train goes through the creepy crawly tunnel. Then it goes under the monster's barbecue. It goes through the spiders' cave then past the haunted forest. Next it goes past the skeletons' party and over the crocodiles' pool. Then it goes out again through the creepy crawly tunnel.

Now read and follow the train on the map.

tower of terror

monsters' barbecue

spiders' cave

witches' kitchen

crocodiles' pool

skeletons' party

haunted forest

6   At the theater!

Song.

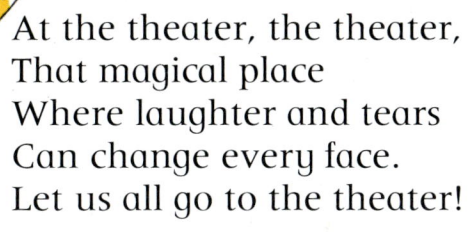

At the theater, the theater,
That magical place
Where laughter and tears
Can change every face.
Let us all go to the theater!

There are actors and singers at the theater.
There is music and laughter at the theater.
There are dancers and comedians, too.
Entertainment especially for you.
At the theater...

51

14

What's your favorite subject?

Listen and look.

It's Wednesday. Ben and Cody are arriving at school.

LATER ...

Practice with your friends.

1 Classes at school

Listen, read and answer the questions.

These children are learning music. How many musical instruments can you see?

This is a math class. How many children know the answer?

These children are learning science. What are they looking at?

This is a swimming class in a swimming pool. How many children can you see?

This is an art class. What is this girl drawing?

These children are visiting a museum for a history class. What are they doing?

2 Do you like history?

Listen and say the subjects.

| math | history | art | science | music | swimming |

Talk to your friend.

 Do you like history?) (Yes, but my favorite subject is art.

Now listen to some children at school. Which subject are they doing?
Listen and point.

3 What's Fido doing?

Read and match.

He's making a mark on the outside of the wheel.
He's measuring things with his wheel.
He's cutting out a circle of paper. He's making a wheel.
He's pushing a stick through the middle of the wheel.
He's rolling the wheel along a line. He's measuring
the outside of the wheel.

4 Snakes and Ladders at school

Game.

Finish

34 | 35 You break a window. | 36 | 37 You fall asleep! | 38

33 | 32 | 31 | 30 | You get 10/10 for math. | 29 | 28

23 You answer lots of questions in science. | 24 | You carry the teacher's books. | 25 | 26 | 27

You are noisy in class. | 22 | 21 | 20 | 19 | 18 It's raining. You can't play outside.

12 | 13 | 14 | Art class. You paint a beautiful picture. | 15 | 16 | 17

11 | 10 Swimming class today! | 9 | 8 | 7 | 6

Start

1 | 2 | 3 You forget your pencil. | 4 | 5 You clean the board.

Phone for a cab

 Listen and look.

Ben's Aunt Kate is going on vacation in France.

Woman:	Hello, Radio Cabs.
Eddy:	Hello. Can I have a cab, please?
Woman:	Yes, of course. What's your address, please?
Eddy:	6 Lime Avenue.
Woman:	Pine Avenue?
Eddy:	No. Lime Avenue. L-I-M-E.
Woman:	6 Lime Avenue. What time do you need the cab?
Eddy:	Now, please.
Woman:	Where do you want to go?
Eddy:	We want to go to the airport. The plane leaves at a quarter after ten.
Woman:	What's your name, please?
Eddy:	Taylor.
Woman:	Can you spell that, please?
Eddy:	T-A-Y-L-O-R.
Woman:	All right. The cab's coming now.
Eddy:	Thanks. Goodbye.
Woman:	Goodbye.

 Practice with your friends.

1 Find the answers!

 Answer the questions with your partner.

1   What is Ben's aunt's name?
2   Where is she going for her vacation?
3   What time does her plane leave?
4   What is the matter with the car?
5   Who does Eddy phone?

15

2 Telephone numbers

Listen and point.

Ask your friend about the telephone numbers.

What is Radio Cab's number?   436-5107

3 Going away

Ask about times.

train station

airport

bus station

boat

 What time does the plane leave?   Eleven o'clock.

4 Who's speaking

 Listen to the conversation. Point to the correct ticket.

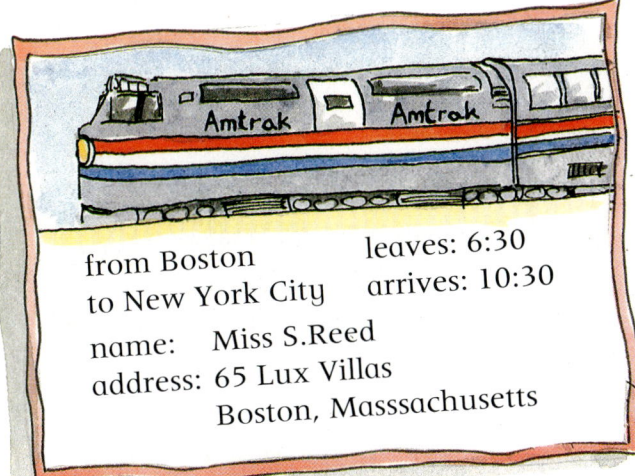

from Boston to New York City

leaves: 6:30
arrives: 10:30

name: Miss S.Reed
address: 65 Lux Villas
Boston, Masssachusetts

from New York City to Paris, France

leaves: 9:30
arrives: 10:30

name: Mrs. E. Sharman
address: 17 South Street,
New York City

from Portland to Halifax

leaves: 9:00 p.m.
arrives: 9:00 a.m.

name: Mr. J. Edwards
address: 43 Park Street,
Portland, Maine

from Manchester to Portsmouth

leaves: 8:15
arrives: 9:15

name: Mr. B. Knight
address: 26 High Street,
Portsmouth, N.H.

5 Phone for a cab

 Choose a ticket. Practice a telephone conversation with your friend.

6 Where are you going on vacation?

 Talk to your friend. Make a ticket.

16 Summer camp

The children arrive at Summer Camp on Sunday

On Monday morning they go canoeing on the river.

On Tuesday they go climbing.

On Wednesday they go on a boat trip.

On Thursday afternoon they ride horses.

I'm going here for my vacation next week. Look!

They play tennis on Friday morning.

On Friday evening they have a goodbye party and on Saturday they go home.

1 What day is it?

Look at the schedule.

Sunday	Monday	Tuesday	Wednesday	Thursday	Friday	Saturday
children arrive	go canoeing	go climbing	boat trip	go swimming	play tennis	go home
	go hiking in the woods	build a tree house		ride horses	goodbye party	

 Listen to Jill and Ben. Point to the day.

2 Find the answers

Talk to your friend.

 When do they play tennis? Friday morning.

have a goodbye party	go swimming
ride horses	go hiking in the woods
arrive at the camp	build a tree house

3 Months of the year

 Listen and say.

January February March April May June
July August September October November December

4 Special days in the United States

 Listen and read.

Valentine's Day is on February 14th. People send cards to someone they love. These children are making Valentine's cookies.

4th of July is Independence Day. There are picnics during this day and bonfires and fireworks at night.

Halloween is on October 31st. Some children dress up as ghosts or witches.

 Answer the questions with your partner.

1 When do people get cards like this?

2 When can you see witches in the street?

3 When do you see these?

 What special days do you have in your country? Talk to your friend.

5   A happy hippo holiday

 Song.

Hippos are always doing things
Like eating chocolate cake.
Hippos are always lying
In the mud at the bottom of the lake.
So now all the hippos are playing,
And to all the people they're saying,
"This is our hippo holiday."

It's a hip, hip, hip, hip, hippy.
It's a hap, hap, hap, hap, happy.
It's a hip, hip, hip, hooray.
It's a happy hippo holiday.

Hippos are always blowing
Bubbles at the bottom of the pool.
Hippos like blowing bubbles,
Because the bubbles keep them cool.
So now all the hippos are playing,
And to all the people they're saying,
"This is our hippo holiday."

6   My ideal vacation

Plan a summer camp with your friends.

Let's play tennis
on Monday.

And let's go swimming
underwater on Tuesday.

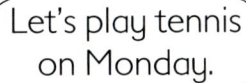

The thank-you letter

 Listen and look.

It's Ben's birthday. The mailman brings a package.

 Practice with your friends.

1 Ben's letter

Read Ben's letter and look at the picture.
Find these things:

A stamp. Ben's address. Aunt Kate's name.
An envelope. Aunt Kate's address. A package.

2   Ben's birthday presents

 What does Ben have? Listen and point.

 What does Ben want? Talk to your friend.

  He has a scarf but he wants a plane.

3   Writing a letter

Which of these things does Ben need to write a letter?

 Talk to your friend.

 Does Ben need a pen?

Yes.

 Does he need any string?

No.

4 Dear Aunt Jane

 Song.

Dear Aunt Jane,
Thank you for the hairbrush.
Mom likes it very much.
And please, dear Aunt Jane, next year send me a car ...

Oh no, Joe! You can't write that!
That's not a proper letter.
Oh no, Joe! You can't write that!
Where's the date? And where's the address?
That's not a proper letter. That's not a proper letter.

Dear Aunt Jane,
Thank you for the hairbrush.
I like the hairbrush very much.
Dear Aunt Jane. This letter comes from Joe.
I like cars too, you know ...

5 Which of Ben's presents do you want?

 Talk to your friend.

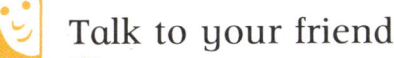

I want some rollerskates.   I don't. I want the spaceship.

 Write a thank-you letter for the present you want.

The post office

 Listen and look.

It's four o'clock. Ben is mailing his letter to Aunt Kate.

 The mailman puts the letters in his box and takes them to the sorting office.

 This machine sorts the letters from the packages.

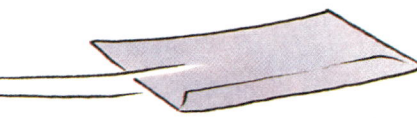

 Then some people put postmarks on the letters.

 These people put the letters into boxes for different towns.

 The letters go to the different towns by train, or truck, or plane.

 In the morning, the mailman delivers the letters.

1 Can you remember?

What happens to Ben's letter at these times?

 Talk to your friend.

> What happens to Ben's letter at four-thirty?

> The mailman puts it in his box and takes it to the sorting office.

2 The letter

 Listen and read.

When you sit and write a letter
And you put it in the mail box,
Do you know what happens to it,
When you put it in the mail box?
Well, the letter takes a long trip,
It travels through the night.
And this is the story of that letter,
The letter that you write.

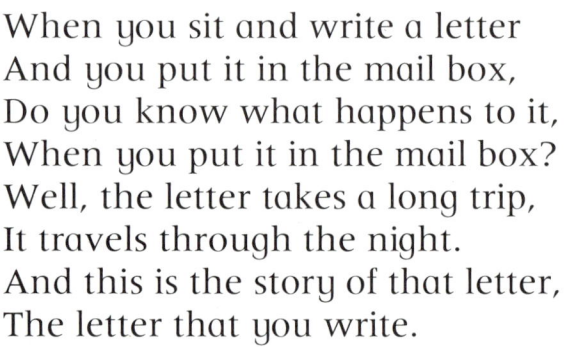

Well, the mailman takes the letter to the sorting office.
He puts all the letters in a sorting machine.
Then the mailman puts the letters into mailbags
And the mailbags take a trip by train, or truck or plane.
And when they reach their destination,
The mailman takes them from the station.
They sort them for delivery,
And they bring them to you and me.

18

3   A day in the life of Fido the Great!

Game. Can Fido the Great catch Mog, the famous letter thief?

11 At nine o'clock he flies to work. Go to the police station.

10

9 He has breakfast at eight o'clock. Miss a turn.

12

15 police station POLICE

16

17

14

13

18 It's eleven-thirty. He sees Will, the car thief. Go back to square 14.

19

38 Very good, Fido!

37 It's eight o'clock. He finds Mog!

36 airport ENTER PASSPORTS

8

7

6 He does his exercises at six-thirty. Go back to the sports center.

21 restaurant EATS

20

35

34 It's seven-thirty. Where is Mog? Go to the airport.

5

22

23

24 He has lunch at a quarter after one. Go to the restaurant.

25

26

33

4 sports center

3

27 It's a quarter after three. Fido goes to look in the park.

32

2

28

It's a quarter after five. He's asleep! Miss a turn.

1 Fido gets up at six o'clock. Go to square 3.

29

30

31

park

Pets

Listen and look.

19

How do I take care of hamsters?

You must have a home for them.

You must keep their home clean and they mustn't get cold.

You must give them food and water to drink.

You mustn't hurt them. You must hold them like this.

 Practice with your friends.

Golden hamsters come from the Middle East. They live in grassland. They have light brown fur, short tails and short legs. They sleep in the day and play at night. They eat fruit, nuts, seeds and very small animals.

1 Which pet are they describing?

 Listen and point.

2 How do you take care of a dog?

 Talk to your friend.

How do I take care of a dog?

You must take it for a walk every day.

3 Whose pets are they?

Read and match the pets with their owners.

Daniel's pet can talk. She eats seeds. Daniel must clean her home every day. Her name's Dot.

Sam's pet sleeps in the winter. Sam must not wake her up. In the summer, she lives in Sam's yard.

Carl must take his pet for a walk every day. He must brush her coat, too. She eats meat and she likes bones for a snack.

Rosie must give her pet milk and fish. He doesn't like dogs!

grizzly bear | Indian elephant

lion | panda

kangaroo | fox

zebra | tiger

parrot | hippo

4 Where do these animals come from?

Look at the map.

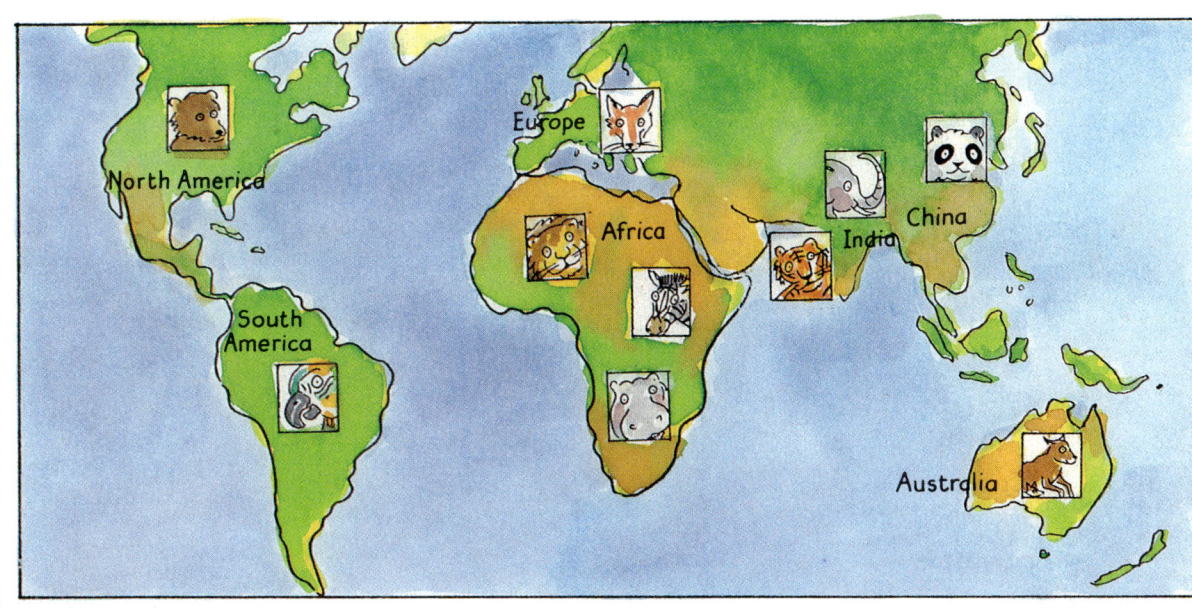

Talk to your friend.

Where do pandas come from?   They come from China.

5 Running wild, running free

Song.

Running wild and running free.
Climbing high in a tree.
Our natural life was so much finer.
We don't like it here.

And the panda is dreaming of China,
Of his natural life back in China.
So what do the elephants think of?
The tigers and the kangaroos?
So what do the animals think of,
The animals living in our zoos?

Once we were . . . once we were . . .
Once we were . . . once we were . . .
Running wild and running free . . .

20 Goodbye!

It's August. Ben and his family are getting ready to go camping for their summer vacation.

Practice with your friends.

1   Where are they?

Look at picture 4. Listen and point.

2   Do they have the tent?

Look at Mrs. Taylor's list and picture 4.
Talk to your friend.

 Do they have the tent?

Yes, it's on top of the car.

What don't they have?

tent
sleeping bags
kettle
frying pan
clothes
beach ball
canoe

3 What do they need?

Look and say.

 They need a kettle. They must take it with them.

They don't need a computer. They must leave it at home.

4 Taking care of the hamsters

Can you take care of my hamsters, please, Cody?

Yes, of course. What must I do?

 Imagine you are Ben. What must Cody do?
Talk to your friend.

5 Ben and Jill's year

Look and read.

September

Ben's school term starts.

October

Jill learns to dive.

November

Thanksgiving Day

December

Jill has a party.

January

Ben makes a snowman.

February

Jill gets a Valentine card.

March

Ben's birthday.

April

Jill goes to summer camp

May

The class visits a museum.

June

Jill goes for a picnic.

July

Ben gets two hamsters.

August

Summer vacations. Goodbye.

Talk to your friend.

 When does Ben visit a museum? In May.

 Draw and write about your year.

Longman Group Limited,
Longman House, Burnt Mill, Harlow,
Essex CM20 2JE, England
and Associated Companies throughout the world.

The original book on which this edition is based
was published as Splash! Pupils' Book 2 in 1993.

First published 1995
ISBN 0 582 25558-9

Set in 14/16 Meridien Infant
and 14/16 Gill Sans Infant

Original design by Ann Samuel
Produced by **AMR**

Illustrated by Kathy Baxendale, Wendy Cantor,
Caroline Church, Malcolm Livingstone, Nina
O'Connell and Charles Whelon

Music by John Du Prez
Music for 'We like eating spaghetti' by Vince Cross
Lyrics by Brian Abbs and Anne Worrall

Printed in Spain by Gráficas Estella

We are grateful to the following for permission to
reproduce copyright photographs:

All-Action Pictures/D.Raban for page 45 (bottom
left); Australian Information Service for page 14
(bottom left), 15 (top left); Britstock-IFA/Bernd
Ducke-Eric Bach for page 30 (bottom right),
/Selma for page 53 (top right); Camera Press/Fritz
Prenzel for page 14 (top left); J Allan Cash Ltd for
page 53 (bottom left); Bruce Coleman Ltd for
page 16 (middle), /J & D Bartlett for page 16 (top
left), /Jane Burton for page 74 (top middle right),
/Fritz Prenzel for page 15 (top right), /Hans
Reinhard for page 14 (right), 74 (top right &
bottom right); Colorific!/Alan Durrow/JB Pictures
for page 62 (middle); Greg Evans Photolibrary for
page 53 (middle left); The Image Bank/Don
Klumpp for page 62 (left), /Lynn M. Stone for
page 16 (top right), 74 (middle left), /Richard
Ustinich for page 30 (bottom left), /Trevor Wood
for page 53 (middle right); The Kobal Collection
for page 45 (top left), /Murray Close for page 45
(middle left); Oxford Scientific Films/G.I Bernard
for page 73; PGL Young Adventure Ltd for page
60 & 61; PhotoEdit/©Tony Freeman for page 69
(bottom left), /©Michael Newman for page 53,
/©David Young-Wolff for page 45 (bottom right),
69 (bottom right); The Photographers Library for
page 62 (right); Pictor International Ltd for page
15 (bottom right); The Picture Cube/©Thomas
Dzialo for page 30 (middle left), /©Spencer Grant
for page 45 (top left), /©Eunice Harris for page 68
(bottom left); Popperfoto Ltd/M.G.O for page 15
(bottom left); Reproduced with the kind
permission of the Royal Mail for page 69
(bottom right, top left & top right); Tony Stone
Images for page 45 (middle right), 74 (left),
/Andrew Elliot for page 49 (middle); Telegraph
Colour Library for page 30 (top left), 53 (top left);
Viewfinder Colour Library for page 74 (bottom
middle right).

Photographs on pages 30 (top right), 30 (middle
right) & 40 (bottom) were taken by Longman
Photographic Unit.